Marco

He's a joke
messing a
always me
if he some
things wro

Waxy Max

He's very sporty and
football mad. On the
outside, he's tough,
but underneath he's
got the biggest heart.

Philippa Feltpen

A real peacemaker, she
helps keep the other
Pens in order by sorting
out arguments and giving
good advice.

Can't wait
to see what
happens this
time!

Squiggle and Splodge

The Scribble twins! They're
both quiet, both shy. Although
they may not look alike, they
do almost everything together.

Enter ...

Squiggle, why are you wearing a chef hat?

Splodge, you'll just have to wait and see!

Pens

Helping you to get to know God more

Hand in Hand

Written by **Alexa Tewkesbury**

Every day a short Bible reading is brought to life with the help of the Pens characters. A related question and prayer apply this to daily life. Written in four sections, two focusing on the lives of Pens and two on Bible characters, young children will be inspired to learn more of God and His Word.

What's inside?

CWR

JESUS, BY MY SIDE

'Call to me when trouble comes; I will save you ...' (Psalm 50 v 15)

The 'This 'n' That' race

Pens' town was holding a 'This 'n' That' race. All the dogs in Pens' town were joining in.

They had to jump over *this* box, and crawl under *that* chair. They had to dive through *this* hoop, and run around *that* bucket.

Sharpy was worried. 'It looks very tricky,' he thought.

'Come on,' said Max. 'Let's practise.'

With a box, a chair, a hoop and a bucket, Max helped Sharpy to practise all morning.

'Well done, Sharpy!' Max laughed. 'You see? No matter *this*, and no matter *that*, I'll always be there when you need me.'

Jesus, our Friend, is with us whatever the day brings.

Have you helped someone this week? Has anyone helped you?

Pens Prayer

Dear Lord Jesus, thank You for being my Helper and my Friend. Amen.

Day 2

Jesus, By My Side

'I will put my hope in God ...' (Psalm 42 v 5)

Race time

The 'This 'n' That' race was about to start. Max was watching Sharpy.

'Hooray for Sharpy!' cheered Max. 'I'm right here with you!'

Off Sharpy ran with the other dogs.

He jumped over *this* box.
He crawled under *that* chair.

'Brilliant!' shouted Max.

He dived through *this* hoop.

'Fantastic!' yelled Max.

But when he saw the bucket, Sharpy forgot to run *around* it. He jumped *over* it instead.

'I've gone wrong!' he thought.

'Never mind,' Max said kindly. 'There'll be another "This 'n' That" race next year. I'll help you practise, and you can try again.'

 When things go wrong, Jesus is still there, ready to help us.

Do you like to talk to Jesus every day?

Pens Prayer

Sometimes things go well. Sometimes things go badly. Lord Jesus, please help me to feel Your love always. Amen.

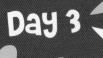

Day 3 — Jesus, By My Side

'Let us keep our eyes fixed on Jesus ...'
(Hebrews 12 v 2)

Tappetty-tap

Tap-tap-tappetty-tap ...

What was that?

8

Tappetty-tap-tappetty-tap …

'There it is again,' Marco frowned.

The sound was coming from Philippa's kitchen. Marco peeped in at the window.

'Hello!' Philippa waved. 'I've been learning to tap dance.'

Marco went inside to see. Tap-tap-tappetty-tap went dancing Philippa. Tappetty-tap-tappetty-tap …

'I want to learn to tap dance, too!' said Marco.

'Then copy me,' smiled Philippa. 'Keep your eyes on me, and do what I do.'

So Marco did. Then with a tap and a tappetty-tap-tap, he danced a few tap dance steps, just like Philippa's.

 Let's keep our eyes on Jesus by learning more about Him to help us grow more like Him.

How can you learn to be more like Jesus?

Pens Prayer

Loving Jesus, I want to learn more about You and to grow more like You. Amen.

Day 4 — Jesus, By My Side

'… [the LORD] listened to me and heard my cry.'
(Psalm 40 v 1)

Every time

tap tap tap tap

Marco was practising Philippa's tap dance in his kitchen.

Tap-tap-tap-tap, he went.
Then, tappetty-tappetty-tap-tap ...

'Oh, dear,' he sighed. 'This isn't right at all.'

'What isn't right?' asked Charlotte.

'My tap dancing,' moaned Marco. 'Philippa taught me all the steps. But now I'm getting them wrong.'

'Then ask her to show you again,' Charlotte smiled. 'Philippa won't mind. She's always happy to help.'

Charlotte was right. Philippa helped until Marco had learnt all the tap dance steps.

'You've got it!' said Philippa. 'And remember, when you need help again, just come back and see me.'

Jesus is ready to listen to us EVERY TIME we need Him.

How do you think Jesus feels when we spend time talking to Him?

Pens Prayer

Thank You, dear Jesus, for Your listening ears. They are always open to hear me. Amen.

Day 5 — Jesus, By My Side

'Trust in the LORD with all your heart.'
(Proverbs 3 v 5)

Splodge's fairy cakes

At school, Miss Fountain Pen was teaching her class to cook.

'We're going to bake some fairy cakes,' she announced.

Squiggle looked pleased.

Splodge looked scared.

'I don't know how to bake a cake,' she mumbled. 'My cakes might look horrible. Or smell horrible. They might not even look like cakes at all.'

'That's why I'm teaching you what to do,' smiled Miss Fountain Pen. 'With my help, your fairy cakes will be beautiful. Trust me.'

Splodge listened very carefully.

Splodge watched very closely.

And with Miss Fountain Pen's help, her fairy cakes did look and smell delicious.

 Jesus is beside us to help us in everything we do.

What would you like to learn to cook?

Pens Prayer

Lord Jesus, please be very close to me whenever I feel scared or uncertain. Amen.

Squiggle and Splodge were looking at the fairy cakes their class had baked.

There were cakes with white icing, cakes with chocolate icing and even cakes with a cherry on top.

'I can't wait to taste mine,' smiled Splodge.

'First,' said Miss Fountain Pen, 'we're going to taste each other's.'

Squiggle looked pleased.

Splodge looked scared.

'Oh, dear,' she mumbled. 'Supposing no one likes my cakes?'

'They will,' replied Miss Fountain Pen. 'Trust me.'

Splodge's cakes tasted yummy. Everyone said so.

'You see?' said Squiggle. 'You can trust Miss Fountain Pen not once, not twice – but every single time.'

 We can trust Jesus time after time, too.

Do you have a teacher like Miss Fountain Pen? What have you learned to do?

Pens Prayer

Thank You, dear Jesus, that You hear my prayers not once, not twice – but every single time. Amen.

Day 7 Jesus, By My Side

'But the LORD … does what is right and never what is wrong.' (Zephaniah 3 v 5)

Window-washing

Gloria's windows needed washing.

'I hate washing windows,' she sighed.

She saw Denzil.

'Where are you going?' Gloria called.

'Shopping,' Denzil replied.

'If *I* do your shopping,' suggested Gloria, 'would you mind washing all my windows?'

'Sounds fair,' answered Denzil.

So Gloria went shopping, and Denzil started window-washing.

'Hello, Denzil,' Charlotte called. 'Come to the park.'

'I need to finish Gloria's windows first,' Denzil replied. 'This is the last one.'

'Would Gloria really mind if you left just one?' said Charlotte.

'No, I'll finish first,' Denzil replied. 'Gloria's doing my shopping, and I said I'd wash *all* her windows.'

 Jesus always did as God asked Him to. He's pleased with us when we do the same.

How many windows are there in your house? Who washes them?

Pens Prayer

Lord Jesus, please help me always to do as You want me to. Amen.

Day 8 — Jesus, By My Side

'… simply obey the LORD and refuse to do wrong.'
(Proverbs 3 v 7)

Glove trouble

Denzil's woolly gloves had holes in them. They let in the cold.

Gloria could mend them. I'll ask her.

When Charlotte saw Gloria, she said, 'Please could you mend Denzil's woolly gloves?'

'Yes,' replied Gloria. 'I'll go and see him.'

But Gloria didn't. She didn't feel like mending anything.

A few days later, Denzil bumped into Gloria.

'Did Charlotte ask you if you could mend my gloves?' he said.

'Erm … no,' mumbled Gloria.

'Oh,' frowned Denzil. 'She said she would.'

Gloria said nothing.

'My hands have been freezing all week!' said Denzil. 'I'm very cross with Charlotte.'

 Telling lies causes trouble. Jesus always told the truth.

How do think Gloria felt when she didn't tell Denzil the truth?

Pens Prayer

Dear Jesus, please help me to always tell the truth and never tell lies. Amen.

Day 9 — Jesus, By My Side

'… how broad and long, how high and deep, is Christ's love.' (Ephesians 3 v 18)

Jesus' love

20

'Does Jesus really love everyone?' asked Marco.

'Absolutely everyone,' nodded Max.

'You're very good at football,' Marco went on. 'Charlotte's very good at singing. Gloria's very good at sewing. Philippa's very good at gardening. Denzil's very good at cycling. So I can see why Jesus loves all of you.

'But why would Jesus love *me*? I'm not good at anything.'

'Jesus doesn't love us for the things we do,' Max smiled. 'He loves us because God made us and we're special to Him. Anyway, Marco,' he added, 'you *are* good at something. You're a very good friend.'

 Whoever we are, Jesus is our Friend who will love us always.

What are you good at? What would you like to do well?

Pens Prayer

Lord Jesus, thank You that You love me for who I am and not for what I do. Amen.

PETER LEARNS A LESSON

Jesus walks on water

Day 10

'… he went up a hill by himself to pray.'
(Matthew 14 v 23)

Time for God

Jesus was with His friends by a lake. He needed some time to be quiet.

Lots of people had been coming to see Him.

He'd been teaching them about God.

He'd been making them better if they were ill.

Now He needed to be on His own for a while. He wanted to talk to His Father in heaven.

'Take the boat,' He said to His friends. 'Sail over to the other side of the lake.'

His friends did as He asked them to. Then Jesus walked up a hill by Himself so that He could pray.

 Jesus knew how important it was to find time to talk to God.

Is there anything you'd like to talk to God about today?

Pens Prayer

Dear Jesus, thank You for teaching me to spend time talking to my Father God – just like You did. Amen.

Peter Learns A Lesson
Jesus walks on water

Day 11

'... Jesus came to the disciples, walking on the water.' (Matthew 14 v 25)

Jesus, the water-walker

When Jesus had finished praying, it was very late at night. He could see His friends in the boat far out on the lake.

The wind was blowing.

The waves flipped the boat up and down.

'Time to go,' Jesus thought.

He left the hill where He'd been talking to God. He stepped onto the lake. Then Jesus walked out on the water to meet the boat.

Jesus, the Son of God, could walk on water!

Do you live near water – maybe a lake, the sea, a river or a swimming pool?

Pens Prayer

Thank You, Lord Jesus, that the Bible shows us how AMAZING You are. Amen.

Peter Learns A Lesson
Jesus walks on water

Day 12

'When [the disciples] saw [Jesus] walking on the water, they were terrified.' (Matthew 14 v 26)

What is it?

The wind was strong. The waves were rough. It was hard for Jesus' friends to row the boat.

Suddenly, they saw something on the water. Something coming towards them.

It was very late. It was very dark.

They couldn't see that it was Jesus.

'What is it?' they cried out. 'Whatever can it be?'

Closer and closer Jesus came. His friends still couldn't see who it was. They were frightened.

'It must be a ghost!' they screamed.

But of course it wasn't a ghost at all.

Jesus' friends didn't understand how powerful He is.

If something ever frightens you, what can you ask Jesus to do?

Pens Prayer

Lord Jesus, You always stayed close to Your friends. Thank You for staying close to me, too. Amen.

Peter Learns A Lesson
Jesus walks on water

Day 13

'It is I. Don't be afraid!' (Matthew 14 v 27)

Peter isn't sure

Jesus didn't want His friends to be frightened.

Straight away He called to them, 'It's all right! It's Me! Please don't be scared.'

Jesus' friend, Peter, was in the boat. When he heard Jesus' voice, he could hardly believe his ears. How could Jesus be walking *on* the water?

'Lord!' Peter shouted. 'Is it really You? If it is, then speak to me. Tell me to get out of the boat. Tell me to walk on the water to meet You.'

Jesus answered, 'Come on then, Peter!'

Peter wanted to be sure it was Jesus.

Jesus is always with us. What would you like to say to Him right now?

Pens Prayer

Dear Lord Jesus, thank You that You promise to be with me today, tomorrow, and always. Amen.

Peter Learns A Lesson
Jesus walks on water
Day 14

'Save me, Lord!' (Matthew 14 v 30)

Peter's water-walk

Slowly, carefully, Peter put one leg over the side of the boat.

Slowly, carefully, he put his other leg over the side of the boat, too.

He let go with his hands. Then, step by step, Peter started to walk on the water towards Jesus.

'Jesus will help me,' he thought. 'Jesus will always help me.'

But suddenly Peter felt the strong wind.

Suddenly, Peter saw the rough waves.

He stopped trusting Jesus and was scared he would drown! He started to sink. Down and down.

'Jesus!' he cried. 'Please save me!'

 When Peter stopped trusting Jesus, he was frightened.

Do you have friends who love Jesus? Pray for them to keep on trusting Him.

Pens Prayer

Jesus, please help me remember that when I trust You, there's no need to be afraid. Amen.

Peter Learns A Lesson
Jesus walks on water

Day 15

'How little faith you have! Why did you doubt?'
(Matthew 14 v 31)

Jesus
saves
Peter

All the time, Jesus was watching Peter.

All the time, Jesus was listening for Peter's voice.

When Peter cried, 'Save me!' Jesus heard him.

When Peter cried, 'Save me!' Jesus reached out and held on to him.

'You don't trust Me very much, do you, Peter?' Jesus said gently. 'Did you really think I would let you drown?'

He led Peter back to the boat and they climbed in. At once, the wind and the waves calmed down. Then Jesus' friends realised how powerful He was.

'You really are the Son of God!' they murmured. And they praised Him.

Jesus wants us to trust Him. He won't let us down.

How could you praise Jesus this week?

Pens Prayer

Thank You, Lord Jesus, that when I call to You, You reach for me – and that when I reach for You, You're always there. Amen.

GOD'S POWER

'Remember how great is God's power …'
(Job 36 v 22)

The most powerful voice

34

'Who has the loudest voice?' asked Charlotte.

'A lion!' answered Denzil. 'Lions roar louder than anything.'

'A bear!' replied Marco. 'Bears roar loudly, too.'

'What about the roar of the sea?' wondered Gloria.

'What about the roar of the wind?' added Philippa.

'What about the roar of thunder?' suggested Max.

Charlotte nodded. 'Those voices are all very loud,' she agreed. 'But the most POWERFUL voice of all belongs to God. God created the whole world and everything in it. When His voice commanded it to be there, there it all was.'

 God's power is so HUGE, He was able to create the whole universe.

Do you have a loud voice or a quiet voice?

Pens Prayer
God of POWER – I praise You! Amen.

Yes. **Oh dear!** Oh dear!

'What's "Oh dear!"?' asked Philippa.

Splodge frowned. 'How can God be with *all* of us, *all* of the time?'

'Exactly,' nodded Squiggle. 'If God's with Splodge, how can He be with me too? And if God's with me, how can He be with Splodge?'

'If I need God's help,' added Splodge, 'what happens if He's already helping Squiggle? God *can't* be everywhere.'

Philippa smiled. 'But that's just it,' she replied. 'He *is* everywhere. God has the power to be with all of us – all at the same time.'

 God's power means He can be with each one of us every minute of every day.

There are lots of minutes in a day. Who do you spend your minutes with?

Pens Prayer
God of POWER – thank You for being everywhere! Amen.

37

God's Power

'… when you give them breath, they are created;
you give new life to the earth.' (Psalm 104 v 30)

Life Power

Gloria and Denzil were out walking. Suddenly …

'Did you hear that?' whispered Gloria.

'What?' asked Denzil.

Cheep-cheep …

'There it is again!' said Gloria softly.

Beside them was a bush. In the bush was a nest. In the nest were some baby birds.

'They're so tiny,' Gloria smiled. 'They must have only just hatched out of their little eggs.'

'We mustn't disturb them,' said Denzil.

'Oh, no,' agreed Gloria. 'But isn't God wonderful? He can give life to something as tiny as a baby bird, and as big as a huge elephant.'

 God's power brings life.

What is your favourite bird or animal?

Pens Prayer

God of POWER – thank You for all the life there is on the earth. Amen.

39

Day 19

God's Power

'My grace is all you need, for my power is greatest when you are weak.' (2 Corinthians 12 v 9)

Again and again

Marco looked thoughtful.

You're looking thoughtful, Marco.

What is it?

'I want to be more like Jesus,' answered Marco. 'But I do things wrong. Sometimes I'm selfish.

'Sometimes I say unkind things.

'Sometimes I don't bother talking to God at all.

'I tell Him I'm sorry,' Marco went on. 'I know He forgives me. But will He *keep on* forgiving me?'

'We all do things wrong,' smiled Charlotte. 'Every single one of us. But God chooses to be kind to us every time we say we're sorry. He will *always* forgive us. He'll *always* help us try again.'

 Our powerful God forgives us over and over again.

Do you ever feel grumpy? When you do, ask God to help you smile!

Pens Prayer

God of POWER – thank You that when I'm sorry, You *always* choose to forgive me. Amen.

God's Power

'But you are our father, LORD. We are like clay, and you are like the potter.' (Isaiah 64 v 8)

Gloria's knitting

Gloria had some wool. There were lots of different colours – red, yellow, green; purple, orange, blue; pink, cream and white.

'I've got so much wool,' she thought, 'but what can I knit with it?'

'You could knit yourself a jumper,' suggested Philippa.

'Yes,' nodded Gloria. 'I'll knit myself a pink jumper.'

'What about the other colours?' asked Philippa.

'I could knit lots of jumpers,' beamed Gloria. 'One for every Pen friend.'

So Gloria knitted each Pen a beautiful jumper that was just the right shape, and just the right size.

When Pens put them on, they fitted perfectly.

 God's power can shape our lives to make them beautiful.

Have you ever seen anyone knitting? Would you like to learn to knit?

Pens Prayer
God of POWER – please make my life beautiful for You. Amen.

43

Day 21

God's Power

'... how very great is his power at work in us who believe.' (Ephesians 1 v 19)

Help in the garden

Splodge had been busy.

She'd helped Miss Fountain Pen to tidy the classroom, sharpen all the crayons and put away new books in the school library.

Now she was ready to sit down and watch her favourite TV programme.

'Splodge,' said Squiggle, 'please come and help me weed the garden.'

'Not now,' Splodge replied. 'I've been helping Miss Fountain Pen all day. I'm not doing anything else.'

Squiggle looked upset.

'Please, Splodge,' she said. 'I need your help, too.'

Splodge could see that she'd made Squiggle unhappy.

'All right,' Splodge smiled. 'Let's get the weeding done. Then we can watch TV together.'

 God's power will help us to be loving and kind, even when we don't feel like it.

Do you enjoy helping out?

Pens Prayer

God of POWER – please help me to be kind and helpful when someone needs me. Amen.

Day 22   God's Power

'... for God everything is possible.'
(Matthew 19 v 26)

Not fair

Marco scored three goals in the Pens' town football match. He won the silver cup.

Max scored one goal. He didn't win anything.

Denzil came first in the Pens' Town bicycle race. His prize was a brand-new skateboard.

Max came third. He didn't win a prize at all.

'It's not fair!' he complained. 'I didn't win the cup, and I didn't get the skateboard.'

'Don't be cross,' said Gloria.

'But I *am* cross!' grumbled Max.

'Then ask God to take your crossness away,' Gloria replied. 'God doesn't want you to be grumpy. Talk to Him and He'll help you.'

God has the power to answer the prayers we say to Him.

Would you like God to help you with something? Why not ask Him now?

Pens Prayer

God of POWER – thank You so much for helping me when I ask You to. Amen.

Day 23 — God's Power

'May you be made strong with all the strength which comes from his glorious power ...' (Colossians 1 v 11)

Sneezy Charlotte

'A-A-A-Tishoo!' sneezed Charlotte.

She had a very bad cold. She'd been sneezing all night.

'A-A-A-Tishoo!' Charlotte was still sneezing in the morning.

'Bother,' she moaned. 'I can't stop – A-A-A-TISHOO! – sneezing!'

Philippa arrived with a lemon and some honey. She used them to make Charlotte a warm, soothing drink.

'I've asked God to look after you and to keep you company while you're not well,' Philippa said. 'I'm going to keep you company, too.'

Philippa read stories to Charlotte, and they shared a box of chocolates.

'Thank you, Philippa,' smiled Charlotte. 'I'm sure I feel better already.'

 When we're not well, God has the power to comfort us.

Have you ever had a bad cold? Did you sneeze a lot?

Pens Prayer

God of POWER – You make me strong when I feel weak. Thank You! Amen.

God's Power

'How wonderful are the things you do! Your power is so great …' (Psalm 66 v 3)

Keeping Safe

Sharpy was feeling naughty. He picked up Max's football boot in his mouth.

'Sharpy!' said Max. 'Put that down.'

Sharpy didn't. He took the boot into the garden.

'Sharpy!' called Max. 'Come here now.'

Sharpy dropped the boot behind the dustbin.

'Sharpy, bring me my boot!' ordered Max.

Sharpy scampered to the gate. He jumped over the top and ran into the road!

'Sharpy, no!' shouted Max.

He rushed outside and led Sharpy back into the garden.

'The road is dangerous, Sharpy,' Max said. 'You must do as I say so that I can keep you safe.'

 God wants to keep us safe with Him forever.

Can you think of something God asks us to do?

Pens Prayer

God of POWER – help me to obey You. I want to stay safe with You always. Amen.

JAIRUS'S DAUGHTER
The little girl who lived

Day 25

'... when [Jairus] saw Jesus, he threw himself down at his feet ...' (Mark 5 v 22)

'Who touched me?'

A man was looking worried. His name was Jairus. He was trying to find Jesus. Jairus saw Him in a crowd of people.

'Jesus,' he said, 'my little daughter's not well. You can make her better. Please come with me.'

Jesus and Jairus pushed through the crowd.

Suddenly Jesus stopped.

'Someone touched me,' He said. 'Who was it?'

'There are so many people here,' Jesus' friends replied. 'Lots of them must have touched You.'

But Jesus was talking about someone who was ill. As soon as that person had touched Jesus' clothes, God's power had made her better.

 God gave Jesus His power to make sick people well again.

Do you know someone who is ill? Ask God to be with them now.

Pens Prayer

Father God, thank You so much for Jesus. He shows us how powerful You are. Amen.

Jairus's Daughter
The little girl who lived

Day 26

'My daughter, your faith has made you well.' (Mark 5 v 34)

Trust in Jesus

A woman was looking worried. She'd heard Jesus ask who had touched Him.

'It was me,' she said. 'I'm the one who touched You.'

The woman was frightened. Was she in trouble?

'I've been ill for so long,' she explained. 'No doctor has been able to help me. But I knew that if I could just touch Your clothes, I would get well again.'

Jesus smiled a big smile.

'You *are* well again,' He said. 'You trusted Me, so God's power has made you better.'

The woman trusted Jesus to make her well.

Have you ever been to see the doctor? Pray for doctors as they help to make people better.

Pens Prayer

Thank You, Jesus, that You used God's power to help people. Amen.

Jairus's Daughter
The little girl who lived

Day 27

'Don't be afraid, only believe.' (Mark 5 v 36)

Bad news

56

A servant was looking sad. He'd come from Jairus's house. He had bad news.

'I'm so sorry, Jairus,' the servant said. 'Your daughter has died. Jesus won't be able to help her now.'

Jesus shook His head and looked at Jairus.

He smiled at him kindly.

'Don't worry, Jairus,' Jesus said. 'And don't be scared. You trusted Me when you asked Me to make your daughter better. Keep trusting Me now.'

Jesus knew that God's power could still help Jairus's daughter.

Do you sometimes feel worried? If you do, remember God's power to help you.

Pens Prayer

Lord Jesus, whether I'm happy or sad, please teach me to trust You. Amen.

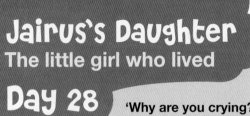

Jairus's Daughter
The little girl who lived

Day 28

'Why are you crying? The child is not dead – she is only sleeping!' (Mark 5 v 39)

Only asleep

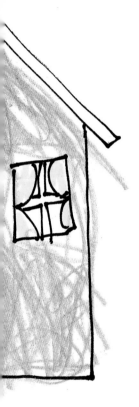

Jairus was looking upset. But he tried to keep trusting Jesus.

Jesus asked His friends, Peter, James and John, to go with them. Together they all walked to Jairus's house.

When they got there, Jesus could hear people crying. Jairus's family and friends were so sad about his poor daughter.

But Jesus said, 'What's all this? There's no need for tears. The little girl isn't dead. She's asleep, that's all.'

Jairus's family and friends found it hard to believe in God's power.

If your friends are sad, how can you cheer them up? Ask God to help you.

Pens Prayer

Dear Jesus, thank You that You are with me, even when I feel sad. Amen.

Jairus's Daughter
The little girl who lived

Day 29

'[Jesus] took her by the hand ...' (Mark 5 v 41)

60

Jairus's family and friends were amazed. They couldn't believe what Jesus had said.

'What are You talking about?' one asked.

'The girl's died. You're too late,' said another.

Jesus took no notice.

He went into the room where the little girl was lying. Her mother, father and Jesus' three friends went, too.

Then Jesus took hold of her small hand.

'Hello, little girl,' He said softly. 'It's time to wake up now. Up you get.'

God gave Jesus the power to bring the girl back to life!

What can you see around you that God has made with His power?

Pens Prayer

Father God, help me to always remember how AWESOME you are! Amen.

Jairus's Daughter
The little girl who lived

Day 30

'When this happened, they were completely amazed.' (Mark 5 v 42)

All better

The little girl was looking very well. She got out of bed. She walked around the room.

Her mother and father's eyes popped wide open!

Their mouths dropped wide open too!

They couldn't believe it! Neither could their friends and family.

Jesus just smiled.

'I told you there was no need for tears,' He said. 'Now, this little girl looks hungry. Go and get her something to eat.'

With God's power, everything is possible.

What do you think the little girl's mother and father said to Jesus?

Pens Prayer

Lord God, You are SO powerful. Thank You for loving me. Amen.

Pens for special times.

An exciting story plus daily Bible-reading notes

Easter

Help young children understand the true meaning of Easter.

by Alexa Tewkesbury

32-page full colour booklets, 148x148mm

Christmas

The *Pens* characters tell the Christmas story to make Jesus' birth real and memorable for young children.

Starting School

Help children start school confidently, knowing that God goes there with them.

Available online, or from Christian bookshops.

For current prices visit
www.cwr.org.uk/store

Visit www.cwr.org.uk/distributors for list of National Distributors.

All Scripture references are from the GNB: Good News Bible © American Bible Society 1966, 1971, 1976, 1992. Used with permission.

Concept development, editing, design and production by CWR

Printed in China by 1010 Printing Ltd.

ISBN: 978-1-85345-693-0

OTHER CWR DAILY BIBLE-READING NOTES

Every Day with Jesus for adults
Inspiring Women Every Day for women
Life Every Day (Jeff Lucas) for adults
Cover to Cover Every Day for adults
Mettle for 14- to 18-year-olds
YP's for 11- to 15-year-olds
Topz for 7- to 11-year-olds

Friends

Father God

Following Jesus

Really Special

Daily devotions for young children

Trusting God

Helping and Serving

Big and Small

God's Book

God's Love

God Cares

God's Heroes

Thank You God

Hand in Hand

Belonging to God

Ideal for children aged 3 to 6

Come on in and meet your new Pens friends! We'll find out how, wherever we go, whatever we are facing, day or night, Jesus will be with us – and we'll help you draw close to God through our stories, Bible readings and prayers.

www.cwr.org.uk

email: mail@cwr.org.uk

to everyday life and

9781853456930

£ 3.99